SCULPTURE

Also by LILLIAN JOHNSON

Papier-Mâché

Sculpture

THE
BASIC
METHODS
AND
MATERIALS

by Lillian Johnson

AVID McKAY   COMPANY, INC., NEW YORK

This book is dedicated to my children
Susan and Eugene

Acknowledgments

I wish to acknowledge my indebtedness to the following for their help toward
  assembling this book:

Genevieve Karr Hamlin, sculptor, for constructive criticism

Alfred J. Hedal, Ron Golcher, Harriet Oyler, and Eugene Johnson, for photographs

Jean Isley, for clerical help

Reuben Porton, of Sculpture Associates, New York, for the use of some of the
  sculpture materials and tools used to illustrate procedure methods.

Contents

Introduction

SCULPTURE, THE DICTIONARY TELLS US, IS THE ART OF CREATING FIGURES OR other objects in the round or relief by chiseling stone, casting metal, carving wood, modeling clay, etc.

But this is what the dictionary does not say—

Sculpture is fun! It is stimulating! It is absorbing!

Sculpture is an art form we can all enjoy. We instinctively shape any malleable material we find in our hands. A child shapes mud pies. Bathers shape castles in the sand. A baker shapes his dough. If this shaping is done with thought and planning; if ideas are created and emotions expressed; if the shapes are expressed in a rhythmic, beautiful manner; then a sculpture has been created.

There are artists who study long and seriously and devote their lives to this absorbing art form. A lifetime is needed to explore, experiment, and develop as a sculptor.

But this book is not for the dedicated artists. This book is for fun! This is for the youngster who wants to be creative on a rainy day. It is for the high-school student who wants to develop his creativity, for the schoolteacher who needs to present stimulating projects to the class, and for the camp counselor who hopes to make camp a creative experience. It is for the house-wife who needs an expressive outlet, for the working man and woman who need a change of pace. It is for the man who should put his tools to work on something besides home repairs. And it is for retired, older people who need a new and rewarding experience in their lives. For all these people there is presented here some simplified technical information about the methods and materials of sculpture in the hope that from these pages they will get the necessary information and stimulation to start on the road to creative success.

To illustrate the various methods, there will be well-known and some less-known but fine examples of sculpture, and some examples by the author.

Technical information can be taught, but creativity must come from within. We all have some, in varying degrees. It develops with use and experimentation. Dare to be expressive. The results will be most satisfying.

You will feel like proud parents showing off your young when you present with shameless pride and delight a finished piece of sculpture that is all yours, created from your imagination and made with your own hands.

SCULPTURE

The Sculpture Scene

SCULPTURE THAT WE HAVE BECOME MOST FAMILIAR WITH THROUGH GALLERY and museum visits, monuments and photographs, has generally been made of:

1. Clay that has been kiln fired (ceramic sculpture).

2. Clay that has been modeled to be cast in a hard material, often metal, such as bronze or aluminum.

3. Wood, stone, ivory, or other natural materials that can be carved.

Today, however, to keep pace with the constant introduction of new materials, and because sculpture, like any art form, is a reflection of its time, many new sculpture forms are being introduced and are fast becoming an integral part of today's art scene. Instead of the massive sculpture we are familiar with, we often see thin, wiry sculpture. Sometimes the sculpture is representative, sometimes completely abstract. Sometimes movement becomes important to the shapes (mobiles).

But whether your sculpture is representative, abstract, massive, or light, mobile or immobile, whether it is made of clay, stone, papier-mâché, or toothpicks, the artistic success will depend on first: *a creative idea*, second: *an awareness of rhythm, balance, and beautiful form*, and third: *the respect for the materials used.*

So You Want to Be a Sculptor!

To be a sculptor, you must first have the desire to express yourself creatively. Then you must decide on some definite ideas. Learn as much as you can about the various materials and how to work with them. And develop good work habits.

If it is possible to get instruction by studying at a school or with a sculptor, do so. It will be a valuable experience. However, if classes are not available, you can teach yourself. Be as experimental as you can. Most materials involved are not very expensive, so try them and let experience be your teacher.

There are a number of good books on human and animal anatomy available through your libraries and bookstores. They can be very helpful for reference when your own knowledge and experience are inadequate. Besides a small reference library, you will find a picture file a useful supplement. Collect all kinds of interesting picture material that might someday be useful to you, either as ideas or as anatomical reference.

As a newcomer to the field of sculpture, you will soon learn that it is very important to observe nature and record the natural facts that can relate to your work. Look at the different shapes and expressions on the people about you. It's lots of fun to watch people in crowds, on buses, walking on the street, reading at the library, etc. Watch their expressions. See the interesting rhythm created by the neck muscles. See how much the character of a person can be determined from the back. Look for the differences between youth and age. See the droop of a weary shoulder, the spring of a youthful athlete, the protective love of a parent.

Keep a pad and pencil with you to make quick sketches. This will help you to remember interesting poses for future sculpture compositions. It is also an excellent way to sharpen your power of observation. Watch particularly for the rhythm and balance of body movement, and become increasingly aware of the wonderful functional bones and muscles that control our shapes and movements.

This is true of both humans and animals. If you have a cat or a dog at home, you have a wonderful opportunity to study the structure of animals. Take trips to the nearest zoo when possible, and sketch the animals in action. Start a home file of good animal photographs which you can find in papers and magazines.

Ernst Barlach. "Singing Man." Bronze. (*Collection, The Museum of Modern Art, New York. Mrs. John D. Rockefeller, Jr. Fund*)

Charles Despiau. "Assia." Bronze. (*Collection, The Museum of Modern Art, New York. Gift of Mrs. Simon Guggenheim*)

Clay

CLAY WAS USED TO CREATE POTTERY AND SCULPTURE AS FAR BACK IN THE history of art as we have records. The reason for this is obvious. The material came from the earth. The most important tools were human hands, and permanence was achieved by baking the clay with sun and fire. This is essentially what we do today, except that our clay comes refined and packaged. We add tools for our hands, and bake our clay in scientifically controlled ovens known as kilns.

ENJOYING THE PLASTIC QUALITIES OF CLAY   Take a lump of clay in your hands and play with it. Twist it. Pull it. Shape it. Often this clay play will suggest an idea. The rhythm and shape can suggest an emotion. There are happy shapes, sad shapes, graceful shapes, dancing shapes, etc. You will find them. It is like finding an old man or a flying horse in the clouds, or discovering pictures in scribbles.

Often the clay play will suggest a sculpture. Sometimes you start with an idea and experiment with variations. If you feel devoid of ideas, just start working. One thought leads to another. A push or twist of the clay can start a whole new trend of thought. You will probably find yourself with so many possible sculpture ideas that you will have to make a choice.

"Laughing Face of Vera Cruz." Mexican, pre-Columbian sculpture in terra cotta. (*Courtesy of The Metropolitan Museum of Art. Bequest of Mary Stillman Harkness, 1950*)

DEVELOPING AN IDEA   Make a small clay figure that will indicate to you clearly the action, emotion, and general shape you would like to get in your proposed sculpture. This need not be more than six inches high. This clay sketch is also helpful if you want to make any changes as you go along. Try it in the small sketch first to see if a change is desirable. Keep in mind that a sculpture composition that is compact in design and has no extended parts is technically the easiest to make, and by far the most fun.

THREE KINDS OF CLAY

Moist Clay   Moist clay is a natural earth clay which makes pottery or sculpture. The clay must be kept in a moist state during the process of modeling, so it is covered with wet cloths and plastic sheets between modeling sessions. The clay must be carefully constructed, dried, and kiln baked to become a piece of ceramic sculpture.

Moist clay is also used as a modeling material to create a sculpture intended for one of the casting processes which will be described. It is a very pleasant working material. When it is soft and pliable, it builds quickly and responds sympathetically to the touch of a finger. As the clay begins to dry, it becomes leathery, and at that stage much careful modeling can be done. If the clay dries completely, it can be used again by wetting it thoroughly and kneading it until it is of a soft, pliable consistency.

Self-hardening Clay   This kind of clay is especially appropriate for school and camp projects. While it remains wet and pliable, it shapes as easily as any moist clay, but when it dries, it dries very hard and does not need to be baked. It is a more expensive clay than regular moist clay, but the added expense is equalized by the elimination of the need of a kiln. Children love this kind of clay, for since they do not have to build the clay carefully, they express themselves freely. Once the clay has hardened, it cannot be reused.

Plasteline The third kind of clay is known as plasteline (it also has other commercial names). It is an oily, plastic clay, and can be used time and time again for many years, for it never dries out.* It does respond to temperature changes, though, for it is harder when it is cold and softer when it is warm. So it also responds to the natural warmth of the hand and becomes softer and more pliable while it is being worked. A good-quality plasteline is always responsive to the touch, and is an excellent medium for creating sculptures intended for casting, or for making experimental sketches for other sculptures. Because it does not need to be kept covered and moist, this material has a distinct advantage for the sculptor who can work only periodically. The plasteline sculpture can be put aside for any length of time, yet it is ready to be worked on without notice or preparation. This makes it particularly suitable for a classroom project, when the students meet once or twice a week. It is very difficult to keep moist clay in condition under these circumstances. Plasteline is more expensive than moist clay, but this cost is balanced by the many times (and years) it can be used.

Because the plasteline remains soft, a sculpture made of it could be accidentally dented or misshapen. Therefore, if you are pleased with the results of your adventure with plasteline, take it to a professional caster to be cast in a permanent material. Or read the chapters on casting, and experiment until you feel able to do the job yourself.

TOOLS There are no tools equal to the ten fingers of your hands. Use them gracefully. Use them daringly.

There are times when tools will be useful and desirable. Here are a variety of useful clay-modeling tools. If you can buy some, do. If not, improvise. Shape some to suit your needs. This can be done with a penknife and any piece of wood. Wire shapes bound tightly to a dowel or pencil will help fill out your collection.

* I am using plasteline that is over thirty years old.

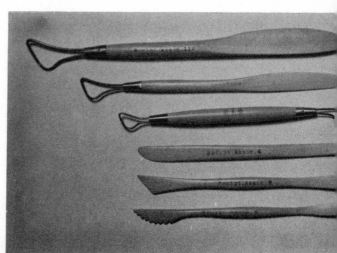

THE WORD "ARMATURE" WILL APPEAR FREQUENTLY IN THIS BOOK. AN ARMA-ture for sculpture is the equivalent of the bones of a person or animal. It is usually made of wire (sometimes wood or pipes), and is a simple stick figure-like skeleton, arranged in the action of the proposed sculpture. It must be rigid enough so that when clay (or any other material) is added to it, it will not sag or collapse.

Not every figure will require an armature. If you plan the sculpture to be massive with no extended parts, it will need no support. If there is no functional need for support, do not use one. But if there is that need, don't try to do without. You can't.

The gauge (thickness) of the wire will depend on the size of the sculpture. Pipe cleaners are sometimes used for very young children and very small figures, because they are flexible and easy to shape. But this very flexibility may make them impractical. An armature should be rigid enough to hold its action, with and without clay.

Buy several gauges of wire to keep available for particular situations. You may use galvanized wire, bought at any hardware store, or aluminum, lead, or composition wires made especially for armatures, bought from a sculpture-supply dealer.

ARMATURE WIRE   3/8   1/4   3/16   1/8   1/16

An armature is easy to make and is very functional, but if it is made incorrectly, it can be quite troublesome. It must be flexible enough to give support without being in the way. There will be little chance for an improper one if you realize that the armature eventually ends up in the center of the clay sculpture. So you must anticipate the final size of the piece. Also, if there is to be a clay base included in the composition, the height of the base must be added to the length of the legs.

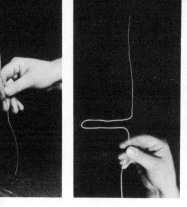

The armature for a figure is made by using a piece of wire a little more than twice the height of your figure. Bend it in half, and twist a loop for a head. Now add the arms by shaping a piece of wire as illustrated, and with a fine wire twist the wires together a little below the loop of the head. This bend will keep the wires from twisting about while you are working. The arms outstretched should equal the height of the figure. Now bend it into action. If you wish to secure your figure to a base, make the armature longer to make loops at the bottom which can be nailed to a board.

For a figure a foot high or over, it is necessary to have more support. Commercial armatures are made with such supports as illustrated. If you decide to make your own, you can assemble a good armature support by purchasing the following at a hardware store or plumbing-supply dealer: ⅛ inch or ¼ inch piping of various lengths to allow for varying heights, since your armature support can be used many times. The pipes must be threaded at both ends. One flange to fit, with screws to secure, the pipe to a board. One elbow, and one "T" joint also to fit. The support will generally enter the body a little above halfway, about the hip area, where it will interfere the least with the modeling and action.

To make an armature for an animal, start with two pieces. Shape them as pictured. Now take one long wire which will bind them together in the center. The loose end of the binding wire will make a tail. Bend it to action. The proportions, of course, will depend on the animal, so a giraffe will have long front legs, short hind legs, and a long neck, while a dachshund will have a long body and hardly any legs at all. Don't worry too much about the

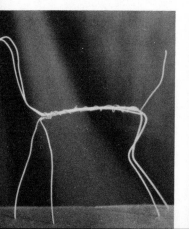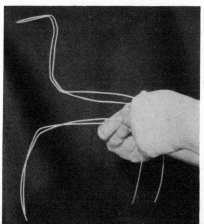

exact proportions, for the important thing is to get the action and to express the personality or the emotion of your creature. Is it a wild cat? An affectionate dog? Or a comical monkey? Say it with clay, but anticipate a functional armature first.

While the preceding information will help you to make an armature, it is neither rule nor formula. An armature can be made effectively many other ways. Every sculptor will find his own pet method.

TAKE INVENTORY

1. You want to create a sculpture.

2. You have a definite idea in your mind; or better, you have made a small clay sketch of your idea.

3. You have the clay and the tools, and an armature if you need one.

4. You are working in a basement playroom, porch, or back yard, so that you need not worry about a piece of clay falling on a good carpet or polished floor.

5. You have a well-lighted workroom, and a table or workbench that is good and solid. Whenever possible, try to work at eye level—so adjust your chair height (if you sit) or have a box or some other means to raise your working area.

6. Turn on your radio. Music will add to the creative atmosphere.

7. Now you're ready. Have fun!

When making a figure, small pellets of plasteline are placed around the armature. Then more plasteline is added to fill out and develop the forms.

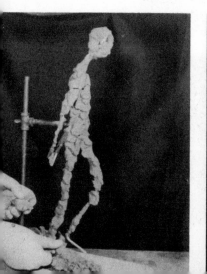

Keep the figure turning and work at eye level. Always keep the development stages the same, do not complete one part before going on to another. (Each part of the sculpture is only as good as it relates to another.) Modeling tools can be helpful after the rough forms are determined. Remember that a simple compact composition, without extended parts, is often the most effective, and certainly the easiest to cast.

In developing this animal composition over an armature, self-hardening clay was used.

The sculpture was developed in one session, so it was not necessary to keep it moist. Self-hardening clay will shrink away from the armature when it dries, causing some surface cracks. This can easily be remedied by filling the cracks with a slip of the same material (a creamy clay made by mixing it with water). Slip also acts as a glue when adding small forms, such as ears, etc. Otherwise the clay is used as it comes prepared, in its moist form. Water is seldom needed, except to keep fingers clean and free of caked clay.

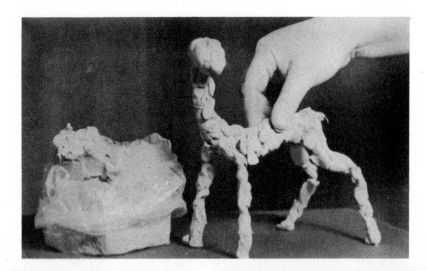

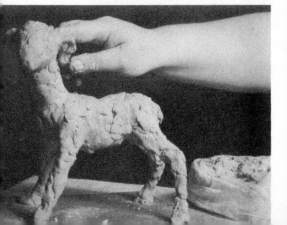

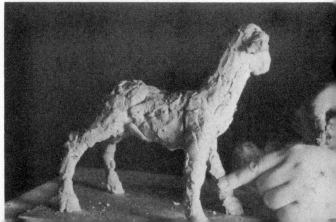

Making a Portrait Head

WHETHER GETTING A LIKENESS, OR CHARACTERIZING TYPES, OR PERHAPS EX-tracting the feeling of a human head from an interesting shape of wood or stone, is your motive, at some time you will probably want to sculpt a head.

For your first experiences with portrait sculpture, try working with clay. A life-size head takes a considerable amount of clay, so don't start one unless you have enough material. Make a smaller one. As a matter of fact, make several smaller ones. They don't need to be likenesses. They can be composites of many people. The best models for people are people. If you feel you don't know enough about the anatomy of the human head, sharpen up your eyesight. Don't be afraid to look closely at heads you see. And don't forget your own mirror. It is often a shock to find that, although we have looked at people about us all our lives, and gazed at our own image from time to time, when we have our hands in the clay, and are confronted with shaping an eye, or lips, or ears, we suddenly don't remember how they really are at all. But don't get frightened. Study them well, work them out in clay, and you will wonder why you ever thought them difficult.

Become aware that it takes more than features to create a good head. The shape of a face is very important and particularly the shape of the back of the head. When doing a portrait, it is essential to get a good structure before developing features. Look at the shape of the jaw. Is it square, round, pointed? Place the ears. See how rhythmic the neck muscles are. Will the pose be straight forward or at an angle? Look at the illustrations on the following pages for different approaches to portraits. Some are molded and others carved, but all are fine examples of sculpture compositions, selected especially to point out the variety of materials, the differences in poses and bases, and the proof that a well-composed sculpture is good when it is a personal expression, regardless of the style and degree of realism.

The usual method of creating a portrait head is to build it of a solid mass of clay, to be cast in another material, such as plaster, cast stone, terra cotta, or bronze.

Determine the position of the head and the composition or plan of the sculpture. Will it include the neck and shoulder? Or will it have a neck set on a base? Will the base be part of it, or will it be mounted on another material? All this should be planned before starting, for major changes are usually more trouble than starting anew.

Ernst Barlach. "Head." Detail of War Monument, Gustrow Cathedral. Bronze. (*Collection, The Museum of Modern Art, New York. Gift of Edward M. M. Warburg*)

Genevieve Karr Hamlin. "Jascha Heifetz." (*Courtesy The Charles Studio, Oneonta, New York*)

Oronzio Maldarelli. "Linda Wu." Saravezza marble. (*Collection of Whitney Museum of American Art, New York*)

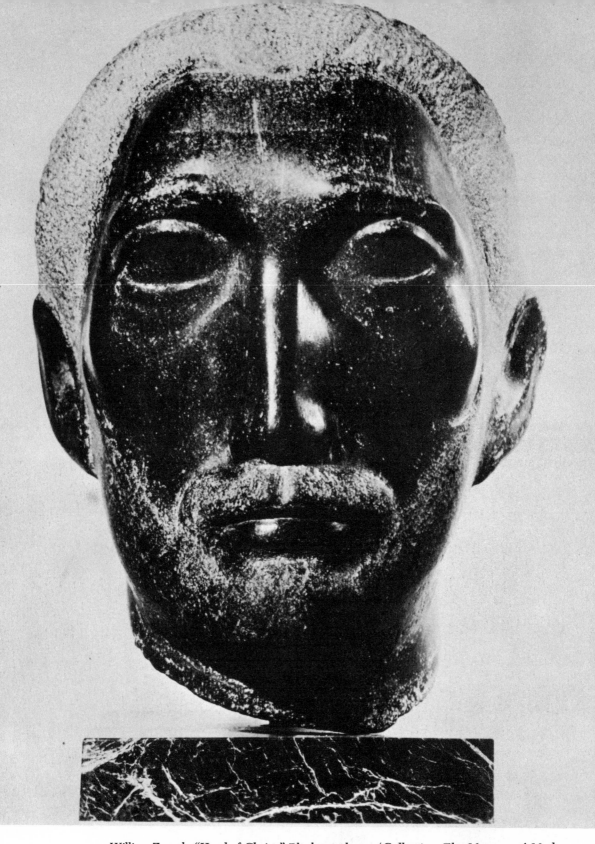

William Zorach. "Head of Christ." Black porphyry. (*Collection, The Museum of Modern Art, New York. Mrs. John D. Rockefeller, Jr. Fund*)

Build or buy a head armature similar to the one pictured. If you work with moist clay, butterflies should be suspended at intervals, to keep the clay from shifting. Butterflies are little crosses of wood tied together and suspended by wire. They are not needed for plasteline.

With the armature set, and the image of your proposed sculpture clearly in mind (or perhaps you have a model or sketches), start building the mass of clay, keeping in mind the egg shape of the head and the angle and balance of the neck.

Now begin to place the features. With clay you can add or take away. If you have a model, study the shapes and relative dimensions. Look at the head from every direction. Look at it from above and below. Keep the shaping basic and simple, and leave details till last. Don't become involved with technique, for if you model the head as you see it and respond to the material naturally, the resulting technique will be an honest one, while a deliberate attempt at surface details can bring only superficial results.

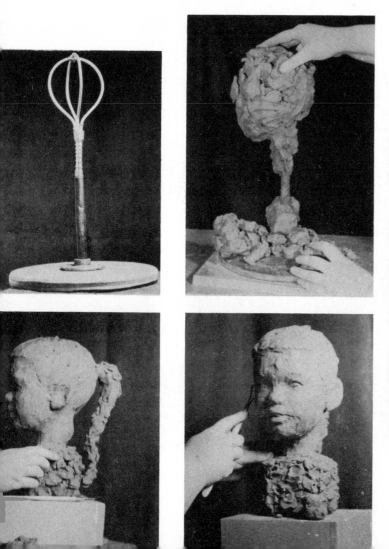

A VARIATION   It is possible to dummy up a shape approximating the shape of a head, so that only a shell of clay will be necessary. This is the only practical way to work a full-size head with self-hardening clay. It is also the practical approach when using liquid metals and other materials that will be discussed later.

The support in such a case is a piece of wood secured to a base with angle irons. There are several acceptable methods to build up a dummy shape. One convenient way is to wrap and tie newspaper to the supporting wood. Then make a shell of clay around it, one half to three quarters of an inch thick. Model the features. When the clay has had a chance to harden, the support and paper can gently be removed, leaving a hollow well-built head which can be mounted on a base. Another way is to make a cloth bag the approximate size and shape of the head and fill it with sand. This is secured to a wood support. The clay is modeled over the sandbag. When the clay is hard, the bag can be untied and the sand will come pouring out.

Carl Walters. "Bull." Glazed pottery. (*Collection of Whitney Museum of American Art, New York*)

Ceramic Sculpture

CERAMIC SCULPTURE IS A TERM PERTAINING TO THE ART OF MODELING A SCULP-ture of clay that is kiln baked for permanence. Many sculptors have delved deeply into the special properties of the various clays, and glazes, and into the best methods of baking.

Because of the intense heat of the kiln, the clay must be carefully built. No air bubbles or bits of foreign matter may be in the clay, lest the heat in the kiln force them out and the resulting explosion damage the work. The sculpture is built hollow or built of a solid mass of clay which is cut apart, hollowed out, and put back together. The sculpture that goes into the kiln to be baked is a hollow wall of carefully constructed clay.

Ceramic sculpture presupposes the use of a kiln of fair size, which unfortunately is often not available to the student sculptor.

Since our purpose here is to learn how to create forms with a minimum of physical problems, and also because the art of ceramic sculpture has had more books written about it than any other sculpture form, we will not delve into the various procedures pertaining to it.

We hope that when you have learned to create with clay, and have gained confidence in your ability to express yourself, you will try some ceramic sculpture. Your library or local bookstore will be able to provide information. Books are also sold at art stores or through art-material catalogues.

Casting

LET US SUPPOSE YOU HAVE CREATED A COMPOSITION IN PLASTELINE THAT pleases you and you would like to preserve this piece of sculpture. Now is the time to learn something about casting.

Casting is the process that will give you an exact reproduction of your clay figure by pouring or pressing a material into a negative mold.

Casting a relief is the simplest casting method, and the most fun. (See pp. 74 ff.)

But the waste mold is a relatively simple process for a sculpture in the round and the most likely method for a beginning sculptor. It will make one reproduction of the clay figure. It is called a waste mold because the mold is chipped away to reveal the finished cast and thus destroyed.

A quantity reproduction can be produced with a piece mold which calls for far more careful planning and skill. Each piece of the mold must be planned so that it will pull away without disturbing the clay. There can be no undercuts to catch the mold. A rubber mold solves the problem of undercuts, and is not a difficult process. However, it is a far more expensive material and would not be practical for large casts.

The cast can be poured plaster, which we will illustrate, or it can be cast stone (see pp. 45-46), or terra cotta. The material you select to cast should be consistent with the design and feeling of the original sculpture. While plaster is not a very interesting material, it is very workable, and there are many ways to make the finished product more pleasing by applying an appropriate patina. (See pp. 43-44.)

WASTE MOLD   We will use this plasteline figure to illustrate the procedure of making a waste mold. The figure is made without an armature since it is massive in design and has no extending parts.

You will need a thin sheet of metal which can be inserted into the clay to form a separating wall. Brass shim, which can be bought at an auto-supply store or through your sculpture-supply dealer, is the best. If no brass is available, aluminum or tin will do. Cut strips of the metal with tin snips. Cut the pieces wedge shaped. Press two or three wedges over or in a half-round form to shape key shims. These keys, formed in the mold, keep the mold pieces firmly locked in place during the casting process.

Determine a good division line which will interfere the least with the forms on the composition. Carefully insert the metal shims so that the pieces overlap slightly to form a solid dividing wall. The clay will need no protection, for it acts as a natural separator from the plaster. This is true of both plasteline and moist clay.

Now get ready for the plaster. You will need a bowl, preferably a rubber or plastic bowl. This is so that if plaster sets in it, the plaster can be removed by just flexing the bowl.

Laundry bluing is used to color the water of the first application of plaster. This is to create a warning signal. When you are chipping away the mold and hit blue plaster, slow up. Be careful! You are almost there!

Plaster of Paris, which can be bought in any lumber yard, makes a fine mold. There are finer ground molding plasters, but they are not necessary for this job. Get plaster of Paris, not gauging plaster!

Now a word about water. If there is no running water where you are working, fill several pails. It always takes more water than you expect. However, the real caution is to those who have running water. Never, never, wash your plastery hands or bowls in the sink. Don't let any plaster in any form get down the drain, or it may set in the pipes and then you have real trouble. So use the water, but not the drain. Keep a cardboard carton to dispose of waste plaster, and to empty bowls, and scrape hands; and a bucket of water to wash hands, bowls, and other working equipment.

Fill your bowl half full with water. Stir in the bluing until the water is a dark blue. Now, working rapidly, and with cupped hand, sift the plaster into the water, distributing it all around. The sifting is to break up possible lumps. Always add plaster to water, not water to plaster. The water will quickly absorb the plaster. When little islands of plaster no longer become absorbed, you have enough. Now with your hand or a spoon, quickly, but gently, stir the mixture. If you stir too vigorously, many air bubbles will appear.

Now take the plaster in your hand and flick it against the clay, getting it as evenly as possible over all the forms. A soft brush will help get the plaster into all the details, or you may blow the plaster to force it into the hollows and to spread it around, while it is creamy. Wash your brush frequently in water. Don't ever allow plaster to set on a brush. I emphasize working rapidly because the plaster will start to set in about ten minutes with no respect for your inexperience. If this should happen, don't fight it. Throw out the batch of set plaster and mix a fresh bowlful. The blue layer of plaster must be applied while the plaster is still flowing and creamy, and should cover the clay with a wall about one quarter of an inch thick.

While the blue layer is setting, mix up a greater supply of plaster minus the color. Let it thicken slightly in the bowl. Now apply it with your hands, covering the forms evenly to make a wall about an inch thick and using the metal shims as guides.

If the metal shims get covered with plaster, scrape them free immediately with a knife or chisel. Let the plaster set thoroughly. It will become quite warm and then cool off. Don't disturb it until it has cooled. Give it an hour or so, or even overnight. Now gently remove the metal shims wherever possible, and very patiently separate the two parts of the mold with the help of wooden wedges.

Then remove the clay, being careful not to mar the plaster with a modeling tool, if it becomes necessary to use one. Wash the mold thoroughly under running water when possible, using a soft brush or a gentle sponge. You now have a negative mold.

There are several methods of preparing a mold for casting, but the most popular method is to saturate it with a liquid soap. Dissolve part of a cake of mild soap or use green soap which you get at a drugstore. Do not use detergents. Brush the liquid soap into the mold with a soft brush. Coat it gently but thoroughly. Wash or brush away excess soap foam. Now coat the whole surface with a thin oil, such as olive oil or lemon oil. Wipe away the excess. Never let any little pools of oil remain in the mold. The soap and oil should include the side walls.

Put the two parts of the mold together, locking the keys in place. Tie the two pieces firmly together with a strong rope. A little fresh plaster will seal the seam and keep the rope from slipping. Or the seam can be sealed with plasteline. Place the mold upside down with the bottom opening on top.

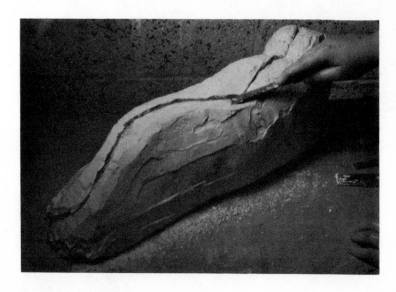

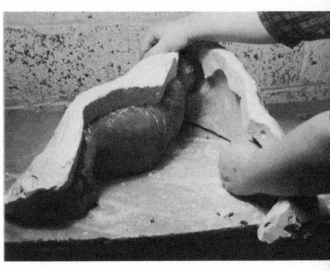

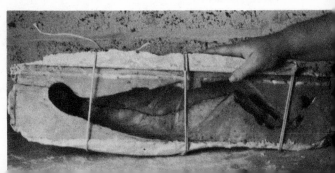

If your sculpture is not very big, you can cast it solid by pouring a creamy solution of plaster into the mold until it is full. Tap it gently while filling it. This will help get the plaster into all possible undercuts, and bring air bubbles to the surface. Then let it set.

However, if you have a fairly big piece, such as a life-size portrait, a solid casting will make it heavy and use up material unnecessarily, so it will be better to cast it hollow. This is done by putting the creamy plaster in the mold, and then tipping and rolling it in all directions, so that the plaster distributes itself evenly about. Do it a bowlful at a time until a wall about three quarters of an inch is formed. This wall is then reinforced with strips of burlap dipped in plaster, placed with a hand through the opening or poked in gently with a rod, when the opening is not large enough.

The next step is exciting and tense, like watching a mystery drama unravel. Will the sculpture that will be revealed be an exact duplicate of the original clay? Or will the villain, impatience, rear his destructive head? If you have followed the procedure described, there is every reason to expect success. But the process of removing the mold to reveal the concealed sculpture remains an exciting experience, no matter how many times you do it.

The mold is chipped away by hitting it sharply with a chisel and mallet. Don't try to get large chunks off at one time. Remove all the white plaster. When you reach the blue plaster of the mold, be very careful, for while plaster accidents can be repaired, the careful removal of the blue mold will virtually eliminate the need for repairs.

Here at last is your plaster sculpture.

Fill in any air bubbles or chisel slips while the plaster is wet. Mix very small quantities of plaster. With a soft brush, drop the plaster into place and shape with the liberal use of water. If you have the unhappy experience of breaking off a piece of the cast, don't despair. Save the pieces. Cut notches in the broken ends, place them together, and fill the notches with fresh plaster.

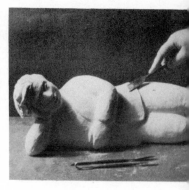

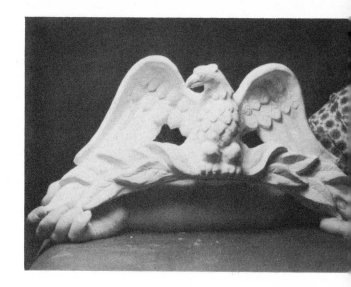

RUBBER MOLD   While reproduction, or casting, is not a creative part of sculpting, it is often the necessary means to an end. Without the knowledge and ability to cast, many potential sculptors would be discouraged. For not all of us have supplies and experience to work with materials that need no casting. I shall assume that any casting you do is to make a permanent sculpture from a clay working model. For that purpose, waste-mold casting is the least complicated, and the least expensive method. Therefore, it has been explained in detail.

However, as we have seen, there are other means to cast sculpture. There is a piece-mold method for careful reproduction, where the mold is kept intact, and thus can be used again at any time, even years later. There is a gelatine-mold process, which is good for quantity reproductions but has a limited life. Or there is the rubber-mold process, which is good for either one or many castings.

The rubber mold has some advantages over the waste mold:

1. The rubber is flexible enough to pull away, even with complicated undercuts.

2. The mold does not need to be destroyed.

3. The rubber mold with reasonable care will last for many years, so it is possible to recast your sculpture at any time.

There are a number of trade-name rubber-mold materials on the market, available through most art-supply dealers. Most of them contain a detailed explanation of the process. The process will vary somewhat, depending on the material. The best advice, then, is to read carefully, and follow the directions for the purchased product. However, it will be helpful to know the general procedure.

The object to be cast is prepared by spraying or painting two coats of thinned shellac over it, allowing each coat to dry thoroughly. The rubber, a water-soluble latex material, is hard on brushes, so prepare a brush by wetting it and brushing it over a cake of soft soap. The rubber is then brushed over the model from the top down, in successive coats, allowing each coat to dry before applying the next. You will know when it is dry, because the wet rubber is milky and the dry rubber is translucent. Be sure to get the rubber evenly distributed over all the details and carefully brush out all air bubbles. Most products call for about eight coats of rubber. Some brands sell a companion product which acts as filler. This is mixed with the liquid rubber and applied over the rubber-coated sculpture for added body, and to eliminate all undercuts. Do not remove the rubber mold from the sculpture for twenty-four to forty-eight hours. This is a curing period. Without this curing the rubber would not be at its maximum strength, and would probably shrink.

In some cases, if the sculpture is very simple in design, the rubber mold can peel off like a glove. But a more complicated sculpture will require that the rubber mold be opened like a coat. In such a case, a razor blade can slit it open along one side. Plan this opening where it will interfere the least with the forms. The slit seam can later be closed with a sticky tape, or rubber cement.

Because of the flexibility of rubber, it is necessary to make a rigid reinforcement, known as a casing or mother mold. This casing (of plaster) is made while the rubber is still in place over the original sculpture. Coat the outside of the rubber mold with a thin solution of shellac, and when it is dry, apply a coat of glycerine. Depending on the shape of your sculpture, make a one- or a two-piece plaster mold which will separate easily, but keep the rubber mold in shape.

The completed rubber mold is thoroughly washed, prepared with a commercial separator or with a solution of glycerine thinned with alcohol, and placed in the plaster casing, which is then tied securely together with cord. Place it with the opening up, and proceed to cast as with a waste mold.

Patina

PLASTER, WITH REASONABLE CARE, WILL LAST INDEFINITELY. THERE ARE EX-amples of plaster sculpture in museums that are hundreds of years old. But the appearance of plaster can be unexciting, for it is a dead-white absorbent material which soils easily. So in order to make the plaster sculpture more acceptable for the home or for exhibition purposes (plaster has no value as an outdoor material), it becomes necessary to color it. Theoretically, the plaster sculpture is created as a prerequisite to future casting in another material, such as bronze, aluminum, etc. For the student, that is seldom accomplished, for either there is no foundry available, or the process is too expensive. And even if these factors were not a consideration, it would be extravagant to cast in metal the development stages of a student sculptor. Instead, the plaster is colored to resemble the material for which it would have been intended. The piece of plaster is colored with ingenuity and inventiveness, with only the success of the piece of sculpture in mind. This process is known as applying a patina.

Creating a patina for a plaster sculpture is a very personal matter. Various sculptors have suggested a number of methods, but even they vary and experiment with each individual piece of sculpture. Patina is a process that calls for experimental imagination rather than formula.

Let the plaster dry thoroughly before applying any color. Then seal the pores with two coats of shellac, thinned with alcohol. Allow each coat to dry thoroughly before applying the next. When the shellac is dry, the sculpture may be painted with thin washes of oil paint, using primarily the earth colors (ochers, siennas, and umbers) and green. Oil paints are thinned with turpentine. Colors may be dabbed in or wiped off in varying tones.

Be careful that the solvents for successive applications are different. Thus, if the plaster is shellacked, the solvent is alcohol. The next coat must be something that has a different solvent. Otherwise the shellac can be softened by the solvent and picked up.

Bronze powders are often used. They may be brushed over the oil-paint washes, or the plaster can be painted first with a bronze solution, and then covered with thin washes of oil color. The bronze powder can also be dusted on over a coat of bronzing liquid, shellac, or varnish while it is still tacky.

Neither the paint nor the bronze powder should be too thick, for it is easy to fill in forms, and lose the original modeling of the sculpture.

Casein paints can be used instead of oil paint. Casein is a water-soluble paint which is waterproof when dry, and is often used as an underpainting for oil colors.

Dry colors can also be used, dusted on while the shellac is tacky.

A very thin wash of red clay brushed into the plaster will make it look like terra cotta. When it is dry, brush off loose powder, and apply a paste wax. This is done to plaster that is not shellacked.

If you would like the plaster to remain white, saturate it with milk three or four times. Allow it to dry between baths. The plaster can then be polished to a marble-like quality.

Painted plaster

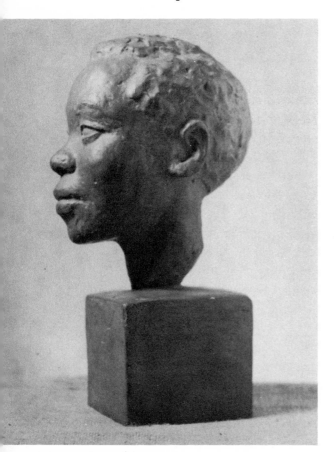 

Cast Stone

A CASTING MATERIAL THAT IS BECOMING INCREASINGLY POPULAR IS CAST STONE. Essentially, cast stone is a mixture of cement and ground particles of stone. Originally, cast stone was imitative. But now the material has taken on a quality and character of its own, which make it highly acceptable for sculpture.

Cast-stone material can be used for direct modeling over an armature, for when it is wet, it shapes easily, and when it is dry, it can be carved, filed, sanded, etc. Cast stone is a stronger material than plaster, and requires no patina, for the color is an integral part of the mixture.

Some sculpture-supply manufacturers make a prepared dry mix for cast stone. But you will probably want to try your own mixtures, so I will suggest some that have been successfully used. If you do not have all the necessary ingredients, try some variations of your own. As long as the proportion of cement to inert ingredients remains essentially the same, you can be reasonably sure of success.

Cast in a plaster mold. The mold must be prepared, first by a thorough soaping, and then by brushing the surface with thin oil.

If the sculpture is simple and small, the cast-stone mixture may be poured in for a solid casting. A weight placed in the opening will force the mixture down to help get it into all the modeled details.

Generally, the mold is cast hollow. This is done by pressing or packing the wet mixture into the separate parts of the mold. This is done until a wall about three quarters of an inch (or more, depending on the size of the sculpture) is packed into the mold. Bevel the edges toward the inside. Let the cement set a while, until you are sure it will not pull away from the mold. Then put the parts of the mold together and tie securely with a strong cord.

The seams are filled from the inside, by packing more of the cast-stone mixture tightly into the beveled edges. Strips of burlap or hemp, dipped in cement, will help reinforce the seams.

Cement must be kept moist for seven to ten days to reach its maximum strength. This is a curing period. Wet cloths draped over the mold, and over the opening, will keep the cast stone wet enough.

The mold is then removed in the usual manner. The cast can be worked on like stone at this point. Modeling may be improved, and seams cleaned with stone tools, files, etc., and the sculpture can be sanded if desired.

SOME FORMULAS FOR CAST STONE   3 parts cement, 1 part marble dust, 1 part asbestos powder, 1 part clay flour. Use colored clay flour or add dry colors. Keep wet for a week to season.

2 parts colored marble aggregate, 1 part sand, 1 part white Portland cement. Season.

1 part fine marble dust, 1 part medium marble dust, 2 parts white artificial stone (get this at dental-supply dealer). This mixture sets overnight and does not need to be seasoned like cement.

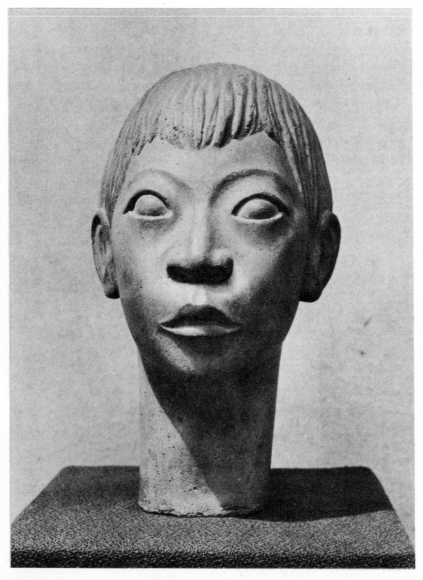

Francisco Zuniga. "Totonac Boy." Cast stone. (*Collection, The Museum of Modern Art, New York. Inter-American Fund*)

Plaster Modeling

THERE COMES A TIME IN EVERY SCULPTOR'S LIFE WHEN HE WANTS TO WORK larger than his supply of material permits.

The solution to that small problem is direct plaster modeling.

The materials needed are simple and relatively inexpensive. With a little experience the resulting sculpture can be anything you want it to be. It can be bold, rough in texture, or sensitive and delicately finished. It can be any kind of expression from realism to complete abstraction.

First, as always, start with a definite idea. Work out a small rough clay sketch to determine the composition, rhythm, and balance. Now assemble the following materials:

1. Plaster of Paris (the quantity will depend on the size of the sculpture you are making). Plaster is less expensive per pound in large bags. It comes in five-, ten-, twenty-five-, fifty-, and one-hundred-pound bags. Be sure to have enough, but keep the bag tightly closed and in a dry place when not in use. Otherwise the plaster will absorb the moisture in the air and lose its effectiveness.

2. Burlap—a loose-weave burlap cut in strips of various lengths and widths.

3. Wire. You will need a variety of wire from stiff to fine and wire screening, fine chicken wire or hardware cloth. Use galvanized or aluminum wires.

4. Tin snips will do a double duty here. They can cut the wire and screening and also the burlap. Keep them with you at all times.

5. Some useful plaster-working tools are pictured here. If you can get them, do. If not, assemble some old kitchen knives, spatulas, etc.

Muster all your ingenuity to build the armature. There can be no hard and fast rules, for the possibilities are so many that rules would be limiting. The

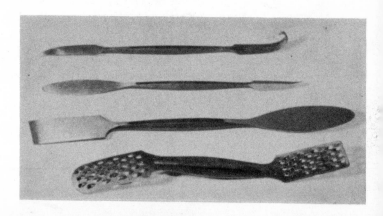

composition pictured here was started with a simple stick-figure armature of stiff wire. Screening strips were spiraled and twisted around to create a hollow form. The screening strips were kept in place with fine wire tied around them.

Before starting with plaster, be sure the armature is right from every view. Is it balanced? Is the rhythm right? Does it convey the emotion you wish to express?

Now, with the burlap strips dipped in a thin solution of plaster, cover the wire, but also shape the forms. The burlap will spiral and twist, and criss-cross itself several times. All the while the sculpture takes shape, the piece acquires a solidity.

The plaster used with burlap must be thin. Until you have some experience, mix a small quantity at a time, for the plaster may begin to set before you have used it all. When it gets too thick, take the remaining plaster quickly, and apply it to the composition wherever it is needed. By cupping your hand, you can apply the plaster and shape the forms simultaneously. Then clean the bowl, mix fresh plaster, and proceed again until the basic forms are complete.

All the while you are doing this, take time, between batches of plaster, to stand back and appraise your work. Keep it turning. Never finish only one part. Work all over, and all around.

This whole process can be a continuous one. It need not be done all at once. So take your time, and do not hesitate to carve as well as build. A form that grows too much need not be an irreparable error. Carve away the excess plaster and then continue.

The plaster can be finished with rasps and sandpaper. The usual carpenter's or cabinet rasp is not good for plaster. The teeth become clogged so quickly, you will have to spend most of your time brushing them clear with a wire brush. The rasps made for plaster have openings for the plaster to pass through, like the old-fashioned potato grater. Get one if you possibly can.

If you are not able to get plaster tools, use an inexpensive chisel, paring knife, or any convenient sharp edge. Keep your cutting equipment clean and dry after each use, or the plaster will dry on them and they will rust and become dull.

Carving

IF YOU THINK IT HAS BEEN FUN TO CREATE SCULPTURE OUT OF CLAY OR PLASTER, just wait until you try carving! Carving is a challenging art form. You have the new problem of creating a sculpture within a given shape and area. It is unlike modeling, which can grow in size and which allows for changes as the work progresses. It is also unlike direct plaster modeling, which can be both modeled and carved, for the wrong cuts can be corrected with more plaster. Carving is an exciting adventure. You must design your sculpture to suit the material. You must become familiar with the material and be flexible enough to make appropriate changes when the carving block dictates it. You must be very deliberate when you carve, for once a cut has been made, it cannot be replaced. You plan more carefully, and you carve more carefully. So, when you have completed a carved sculpture, you really feel like a conquering hero.

Although wood and stone carving are the ultimate goals, it may not be either possible or practical for your first experience. There are situations where it would not be wise to start with wood or stone. The sculptor may be too young, or he may lack equipment. Or, as often happens in group work, there may be insufficient funds. It would be a shame to eliminate a carving experience for any of these reasons. Since it is important to encourage the creative experience and develop the interest in sculpture, it becomes important to be able to improvise or substitute materials and equipment as the situation arises.

Then, as the interest grows with experience, the sculptor goes on to work with more permanent and, in the long run, more satisfying materials. Don't ever forget that whether you use fine marble, glass foam, plaster, or beautiful hard woods, you are a creative artist. You will use your materials effectively, within their own limitations, to create a three-dimensional statement in the most beautiful manner you possibly can.

Wood Carving

CLAY MODELING AND CARVING ARE REVERSE PROCESSES.

When you model a figure in clay, you start with nothing and work toward the completion of an idea. However, when you carve a block of wood or stone (or any of the other materials that will be suggested), the idea will be encased somewhere within the material. You must then chip away the excess material until the completed sculpture is revealed.

Thus clay modeling is an adding process. Carving is a taking-away process.

Carving is a sculpture field that is seldom started before the high-school level.

As a classroom project, it requires space and equipment. A desk is not a good carving table. A good sturdy workbench is desirable. Tools must necessarily be sharp, so the teacher must be constantly alert and cautious. However, excellent carvings have come from creative, sculpture-minded students.

Carving is a favorite sculpture form among adults. For one thing, when a carving is done, it is done. It is ready to take its place in the home, garden, or gallery. There is no kiln needed. There is no casting process. It is complete.

Imagine! You start with a log of a felled tree or a block of wood from a lumber yard, and you end with a piece of sculpture!

There are two approaches to wood carving:

1. You have a definite idea for a piece of sculpture. You make a small clay sketch to define the composition, rhythm, balance, and general proportions. With these facts in mind, you look for a piece of wood, not only the right size, but with the character and color to express your idea.

2. You have an interesting piece of wood. It has an intriguing shape and a beautiful grain. Keep this piece of wood where you can see it often. Turn it frequently. Look at it in all lights. Suddenly one day the wood will suggest to you a piece of sculpture that will be exactly right for it. You will visualize clearly the forms within the confines of that wood, and hardly be able to wait until the excess wood is carved away.

WORKBENCH   Since wood is carved by hitting a chisel or gouge into the wood with a mallet, the wood must be secured in some way, or it will move away with each blow, and you will have no control over your cutting. At the same time, since sculpture is an art in the round, it is necessary to be able to turn your wood often as you work. You should have a strong, sturdy bench to work on. It should be equipped with a vise or clamps to hold your wood in place. Fortunately, many school shops are equipped with such benches. But one is not likely to be found in the average home. Although this often presents a problem to the aspiring home sculptor, there are a number of ways to improvise. Make, or have made, a small sturdy reinforced bench. Buy a vise. A metal vise will have to be lined with wood strips or leather, for the metal vise will bite into your wood, and leave unwanted marks. If you have no vise, nail two pieces of two-by-four securely to your bench at right angles. This will give you something to hit up against and will stop your wood from riding around. If none of these are available, it is possible to set your wood on a sandbag. This is a procedure often used for stone carving, and while it is not ideal, it is one solution for keeping your wood anchored down.

TOOLS   Good tools are necessary. You can start with a minimum number, but buy good steel tools and take good care of them. Wood-carving and stone-cutting tools should be bought from an art-material store, or through a sculpture-supply dealer. (See list of sources on page 92.)

Three good tools to begin with are a flat chisel, a shallow gouge, and a deep gouge. You will want to increase your supply eventually to include other shapes and sizes. You will need a mallet to drive the tool into the wood.

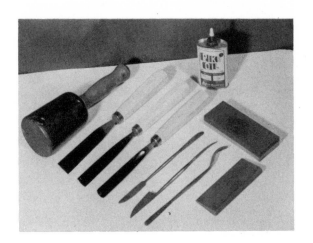

Mallets are made of hickory, maple, and lignum vitae.

Good cutting tools must be kept sharp. Keep a sharpening stone handy at all times. To sharpen a tool, keep the bevel of the tool flat against the stone and rotate the tool against it. A thin oil (pike oil) will help this process. Then turn the tool and remove the metal burr by going over it slightly with the stone. A gouge must be constantly turned while the bevel remains flat against the stone. A stone slip with a curved edge will remove the burr.

A few choice rasps will complete your supply of tools.

A word of caution: Always direct your cuts away from you, so that if the tool slips you will not cut yourself. And when using a tool without a mallet, *always, always, and always* keep your supporting hand behind the cutting tool. If this habit is acquired right from the start, there will be no cut fingers. Then sculpture will be fun; not blood, sweat, and tears.

KINDS OF WOOD   There is wood all around us. The carpenter leaves pieces of two-by-fours. A fallen tree is cut up for firewood. Lumber yards are all over the country. Friends and acquaintances will come forth with offers of wood as soon as they learn of your interest. Take advantage of any good piece of wood you can get. Start a stock pile for future ideas. But before you devote many hours of carving to a piece of wood, make sure it is sound and worth the effort. Become acquainted with different woods and their value to sculpture.

The best carving wood is aged. Freshly cut, or green, wood is likely to split or check as it dries. If you get some logs or pieces of oak, cherry, apple, or any locally available wood, tuck them away in a dry spot in your garage or basement. A coating of shellac or wax, especially on the ends, will help

Genevieve Karr Hamlin. "Pony Colt." Rosewood. (*Courtesy of Charles H. Tipple, Oneonta, New York*)

Brazilian rosewood

Birch

Lignum vitae

Ebony

Mahogany

Walnut

Pear

Apple on lignum vitae

keep them from drying too rapidly, which is usually the cause of splitting. Avoid extreme temperature and humidity changes.

Soft woods are not particularly good for carving. There are some exceptions. Some pines, such as sugar pine, can be carved. Cedar is one of the choice exceptions, for it is easy to get, and although soft, cuts clean, has wonderful color and a pleasant scent. It is a very good wood for beginning sculptors. Cypress knees make good wood carvings. The wood cuts easily and clean. The cypress knees come in fascinating shapes which practically create their own compositions.

Some hard woods are sometimes available at lumber yards, but seldom in much dimension. Many wonderful and exotic hard woods are imported from South America and Africa for fine furniture making. Sometimes pieces of these woods are made available to sculptors. If you cannot buy any in your area, write to some of the dealers listed on page 92 for a catalogue that will describe the woods and list their prices.

Some hard woods that are frequently carved:

APPLE   Light to golden yellow. Beautiful polish.

BIRCH   Domestic, light-colored wood. Clean cutting. Nice grain.

CHERRY   Close grained. Reddish color. Excellent.

EBONY   Jet black. Some varieties have a brown grain. Tricky but very beautiful.

LIGNUM VITAE   Extremely hard. Outer wood light in color. Heart of the wood very dark. Not recommended for beginners.

MAHOGANY   One of the softer, easy-to-cut hard woods. Varies in color from light tan to red.

OAK   Very hard. Strong grain. Demands simple massive design.

ROSEWOOD   Beautiful grain. Deep red brown, almost purple. Very hard. Cuts to a polish.

TEAK   Good clean-cutting wood. Beautiful brown finish. Dulls tools.

WALNUT   Excellent for carving. Lovely grain. Beautiful polish. Brown color.

PEAR   Good for carving. Red brown color. Matte finish.

PADAUK   Similar to mahogany in grain. Hard. Deep red.

MAPLE   Close grained. Light brown. Sometimes reddish brown.

TAKE INVENTORY

1. You have an idea for a wood carving.

2. The piece of wood is ready and waiting.

3. The tools are available and sharp.

4. There is a good sturdy bench to work on. The chips will fly, so you are working in a place that can easily be cleaned up. There is a broom and dustpan handy.

5. You're wearing a smock or old clothes.

6. The light is good.

Well! What are you waiting for? Start cutting.

GENERAL PROCEDURE FOR CARVING WOOD   Draw the composition on the wood with a chalk or crayon. Some woods have a strong grain. It is important to plan the composition so that the grain will curve around the forms you want to emphasize. In a cut block, one side has a curved grain and one side a long grain. A log will have a curved grain all around. You can determine the direction of the grain from the crosscut ends or by making some experimental gouge cuts.

Mark the center of the top and bottom with a crayon. This will help keep the forms balanced.

A clay sketch will help you to place the forms. Secure the wood in a vise. With your largest gouge, start cutting away the wood. Always work from the high points toward the end. Cut with the grain in a swooping stroke. A sharp gouge can cut across the grain, but under no circumstances should you cut against or into the grain. You will recognize a wrong cut by the hollow splitting sound it makes. If this occurs, stop cutting at once, and turn your wood or tool in the other direction. The tool is held firmly with the beveled side against the wood, and struck with a wooden mallet, as pictured.

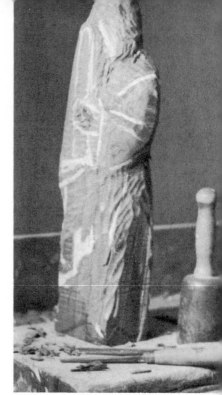

Always cut forms, never hollows. The forms can be carved smaller, but hollows cannot be filled. You will find that as the forms are developed, the right concaves appear.

Check often to see that the wood carving has the rhythm and balance you want. Turn the wood frequently while carving to keep the development stages about the same. Never finish one part and then go on to another. Each part is only as good as it relates to the whole. So work all over and all around.

Allow yourself some time for meditating. Between carving sessions, keep the partly finished sculpture where you can look at it many times and in different lights. Make mental notes of changes, or keep a crayon handy to mark the wood when a change of form occurs to you. Often when you wake up in the morning and look at it with fresh eyes, you can see clearly what you have done well and what you can improve.

Wood can be finished in many ways. Often a very handsome powerful sculpture is complete as soon as the forms are revealed, and the marks of the tools are left just as they are. Sometimes a wood carving is partly smoothed, and partly rough. Sometimes the wood is completely polished. Some woods polish better than others, revealing the color and grain most elegantly.

A wood carving with the textured marks of the gouge can be finished with a protective coat of paste wax, or oil polish.

To finish a wood carving with a fine polish, first rasp the forms to remove the gouge marks, and then finish with sandpaper. All the time you must be thinking about and improving the forms. Use the rasp and sandpaper as tools, not just as superficial smoothers, or you will lose some of the forms.

Sandpaper comes in varying grades from coarse to very smooth. It is used in that order. Buy a good-quality sandpaper. It is an economy in time. Not only does it cut quicker and better, but it leaves a cleaner finish. An inexpensive sandpaper can leave surface scratches.

When the wood is rasped and sanded to your satisfaction, it can then be polished. There are a number of polishes and waxes that you can use. Most waxes and polishes will make some color change on the wood. A clear wax darkens it only slightly. An oil polish can darken the wood considerably. You will have to experiment with the wood where it won't show, or try various finishes on another similar piece of wood, to determine which will be most effective. Decide if your carving will look better with a high polish and just how much color change you want. The color can be a very important part of the final expression.

You can use a commercial paste wax that is used for floor polishing, or commercial furniture polish.

A good homemade polish is made of equal parts of linseed oil, turpentine, and vinegar. This will darken the wood, so use it only when this is desirable.

Stone Carving

LIKE CARVING WOOD CARVING STONE IS A MATTER OF TAKING AWAY THE EXCESS stone to release the sculpture that you, the creative artist, have visualized within the confines of a piece of stone. Again as in wood carving, there are two approaches to stone carving.

1. You may acquire an interesting, unusual-shaped piece of stone. Keep it where you can see it frequently. After a while the color, shape, and quality of the stone will practically dictate a sculptural composition. The very nature of the stone will demand a simple broad design, compact in composition. Even if you should make the error of planning an intricate overdetailed design, you will soon find yourself simplifying, eliminating unnecessary details, and doing what comes naturally, when carving stone.

2. Another method is to design the sculptural composition first, and then look for a piece of stone to fit the size, color, etc.

When possible, acquire some small pieces of various kinds of stone and experiment. Do not get too ambitious at first. Get a minimum collection of stone-carving tools, and several pieces of different stones, not too hard, and enjoy the experience of creating beautiful forms. Learn the possibilities—and the limitations—of the various stones. Don't violate these limits.

Your sculptural experiments can be representative compositions, or purely abstract forms, or a personal variation of either. Whatever it is, it should be an honest reaction to the material at hand, and not a literal copy of a previous clay modeling.

In spite of this warning, however, a clay sketch can be a valuable help to the stone carver, if properly used. For the general plan of the proposed sculpture can be worked out three dimensionally, with rhythm and balance determined. In the clay stage, you can experiment with changes and variations. This sketch can be small, but proportioned to fit the proposed piece of stone. When you are pleased with the sketch and ready to carve, it will serve another useful purpose. The sketch will determine the high points of the design, and thus help to place them in the stone. But don't bind yourself to the clay sketch too literally. Finish the sculpture with the dictates of the stone to guide you.

John B. Flannagan. "Elephant." Bluestone. (*Collection of Whitney Museum of American Art, New York*)

Jose de Creeft. "The Cloud." Green stone. (*Collection of Whitney Museum of American Art, New York*)

Cesare Stea. "Mother and Child." Marble.

KINDS OF STONE   There are many varieties of stone that are suitable for sculpture, from soft alabaster to very hard granite. It is inadvisable to experience your first carving on one of the harder resistant stones such as granite. In fact, it could be sheer folly, for technical difficulties can discourage the creative urge. This is not to condemn hard stones as sculpture media. Not at all. Many of our most beautiful sculptures have been carved from granite. Because it is so resistant to weather, granite makes some of our best monuments. But reserve the experience until you have tried some of the easier-to-cut and medium-hard stones. Become familiar with the methods of working. Learn how to handle the tools, and primarily, when planning a stone composition, think in terms of stone and not clay.

If you live in an area where marble is quarried, you have no problem at all. Often odd-shaped pieces are available at no cost. This is true also of the various limestones.

Limestone is a soft stone, easy to carve. It does not take a polish. Limestones come in various colors, but are most frequently gray and buff. While limestone is quarried throughout the United States, many sculptors prefer a limestone that is imported from France, named Caen stone (after the city Caen, near where it is mined). If the limestone sculpture will be placed outdoors, it will have to be weatherproofed. A weatherproofing solution can be bought from a building-supply dealer.

Marble is one of the most frequently carved stones. It is more durable and resistant to weather than limestone, and softer and therefore easier to carve than granite. Marble is quarried in many states in the United States and also imported from other countries, particularly European ones. Marble comes in many colors, from the beautiful white marbles of Vermont, to the pink marble of Tennessee, to the jet black of Belgian marble. There are also marbles in blues, greens, and grays, and shades and variations, some solid color and some with elegant graining. These marbles vary a great deal in their degree of hardness, so unless you have access to pieces of marble free, and can afford to experiment, when you order a piece of marble for carving, inquire first as to its degree of hardness. Get expert advice.

Soapstone is a very soft carving stone which feels very much like a piece of soap when you rub your hand against it. Soapstone carves easily and can be polished very much like marble. It comes in various colors. Soapstone is generally available only through a sculpture-supply dealer. It is sold in cut pieces or boulders, and the price is determined by weight.

African wonderstone, like soapstone, is purchased through a sculpture-supply dealer in blocks. It is a dark-gray stone that carves easily and takes a high polish.

Alabaster is a soft carving stone that generally comes in a translucent white and opaque pink. Most of our finest alabaster comes from Italy.

While soapstone, wonderstone, and alabaster are excellent materials for a student carver, because they present minimum physical problems, the finished sculptures are good only for indoor use. These stones will not last long in the elements. The carver will also have to control his cutting blows, for while a hard marble or granite requires sharp blows to remove the excess material, a similar blow on a soft stone will leave unwanted fracture marks or bruises deep in the stone which cannot be polished away.

TOOLS   While it is very nice to have a large collection of stone-carving tools, it is not essential. Three or four tools and a hammer, creative imagination, and some energy can produce a fine piece of sculpture out of a piece of stone. Unlike wood, which is carved with a scooping motion, stone is generally carved by direct cuts into the material to shatter away the unwanted stone. For this purpose a point is used. A great deal of the rough carving can be done with a point. The point is also used to remove large chunks of material. When the point has done its job, a toothed chisel is used to shape the forms. This chisel can virtually finish the job, except for the surface texture. When the texture the toothed chisel leaves is not desirable, a

straight-edged or flat chisel will shave the furrows and can further develop the forms. The stone can then be polished. The hammer employed to strike the tools is a short-handled, rectangular steel hammer or a soft metal hammer which is used on certain stones to cushion the blows.

When carving one of the softer stones, it is advisable to omit the use of the point completely. The carving can be done with the toothed and flat chisels. A few experimental cuts on the piece of stone ought to be enough to determine which tools will work best. Stone-cutting tools are tempered differently for stones of varying hardness, so if you graduate into carving granites and other hard stones, check on the temper of your tools. A local monument maker for tombstones or a blacksmith can help you.

To carve a stone, place it on a sturdy reinforced bench or table. Sometimes the stone is heavy enough to keep steady by its own weight. When this is not true, the stone can be kept from moving about by placing it on sandbags. A strong reinforced barrel, either filled with sand or covered with a sandbag, makes a fine work surface.

POLISHING   A polished stone can be a thing of great beauty. The texture and color of the material are displayed at their fullest elegance. To my mind, a piece of sculpture is most successful when the piece practically begs to be touched, and a beautiful piece of polished stone is most inviting. Polishing alone will not make a beautiful sculpture. The basic concept, and the forms that follow, create the beauty. The polishing merely enhances it.

Not every stone can take a polish. And indeed not every stone sculpture should be polished. A polished surface could be completely wrong for one piece of sculpture, which because of the emotion it is trying to portray, should be left the texture of the toothed chisel, or partly so, while another piece of sculpture could better show the beauty of form by polishing the material. The decision must be related each time to the piece of sculpture on hand. Experience, again, will be your best teacher.

Polishing a piece of stone takes much energy and patience. Essentially it is a matter of rubbing the stone with abrasives (which can be Carborundum or another piece of the same material as that used for the sculpture) while keeping the stone wet. The final polish is achieved by rubbing with a soft cloth and tin oxide or putty powder.

There is much more that could be told and much information available for you to read, but the best possible teacher is experience. Do not expect every attempt to be a masterpiece. Work for the sheer joy of accomplishment. You will soon find out if stone carving is your niche in the sculpture field.

TAKE INVENTORY

1. You think it would be great fun to carve a sculpture out of a piece of stone. It's a real challenge.

2. There are several pieces of different kinds of stone and some stone-carving tools available.

3. You do some experimental carving to get acquainted with the material.

4. There is one piece of stone exactly suitable for the sculpture you have in mind.

5. There is a good solid bench to work on, or a barrel filled with sand.

6. You're working outdoors or in a studio or basement, because the stone chips and dust will fly in all directions.

7. You must remember to protect your eyes from flying stone, so you wear goggles.

8. The challenge awaits you!

Other Carving Blocks

PLASTER   Plaster can be poured into a cardboard box or milk carton. When the plaster has set, the container can be peeled off, and the plaster block is ready to be carved. Plaster can be carved with an inexpensive wood chisel. The first cutting, to block out the forms, is usually done by striking the chisel with a mallet. Then the mallet is put aside, and the chisel is guided by hand. Don't forget to keep the supporting hand behind the chisel. If the plaster gets too dry, wet it. Water will not hurt the plaster, but it can rust tools. So dry your tools carefully after each working session. The finer forms can be carved with smaller wood-carving tools, or plaster tools, and the finished piece can be left with the tool marks (often a very interesting texture) or sanded and polished.

Plaster can be combined with a number of materials. Vermiculite, a mineral used for insulation and gardening, combined with the dry plaster, gives a very interesting color and texture to the plaster block. It is reminiscent of Mayan sculpture. Asbestos powder can be combined with the dry plaster to give the block a slightly gray color, and it makes the plaster softer to carve. Some other materials that can be used with plaster are sand, marble dust, ashes, and mica flakes. Sometimes several of these ingredients are used.

Since none of these materials are expensive, it is a good idea to determine the quantity to add through experimentation. For a classroom project, it would be wise to make a number of plaster blocks with various formulas. Label them, and record the ingredients. You can then determine for future use which were the most effective.

Plaster

Soap

Carving a plaster block is really a fun project. There is no hard work, so the forms emerge quickly and easily. Since the material is inexpensive, the carver is likely to experiment. One carving can lead easily to another. The only working problem it presents is one of cleaning. If the plaster gets on the floor, it will track all over the rest of the house or school, or wherever you may be working. So work out of doors whenever possible, or in a basement or studio that can be swept.

SOAP Soap can be carved with a knife or with a modeling tool. The cake of soap should be soft and fresh. Charming small sculpture can be made. The sculpture should be designed so that there are no fragile extended parts, for they can break off. Soap sculpture is necessarily limited in size. However, although it is fragile, with care the sculpture can last many years. Spray the finished work with several coats of thin clear lacquer to preserve the fresh-cut look and color of the soap.

GLASS FOAM Glass foam is a relatively new material made for insulation purposes. It looks like a cushion of millions of tiny black bubbles. The texture is delightful. Glass foam comes in blocks. The blocks can be cut into smaller pieces to suit your purpose by sawing or by using a knife with a sawing motion. The material cuts easily (almost too easily) and has an unpleasant odor (which you get used to). But in spite of these disadvantages, it is an exciting sculptural experience. Glass foam lends itself especially to abstract and semi-abstract sculpture. The glass foam can be cut with a knife, and forms can be rounded with a rasp.

Glass foam

While the finished carving can be very exciting in form, color, and texture, the very nature of glass makes it fragile. So keep it in a safe place. A spraying of shellac or lacquer will make the piece a little less brittle.

There is another way to use glass foam which takes advantage of the fact that it is easy to carve. A sculptural composition can be carved out of glass foam, and this can be used as a core or armature for an aluminum (plastic metal) sculpture. Actually it makes a very good core, for it is light and porous. It could also make a core for a sculpture made with self-hardening clay, plaster, etc.

SALT BLOCKS   Salt blocks, which are bought at a feedstore and used for animals to lick in the pastures, make delightful carving blocks. They come in several colors, and about the size of a brick. They can be carved easily with knives, tools, and rasps. The color and texture are very pleasant. On the negative side, is one problem. Salt absorbs moisture.

If you keep it in a moist place, the sculpture will become wet and eventually melt itself away. So keep it in a dry place and enjoy the experience of carving salt.

Genevieve Karr Hamlin. "Toscanini."

Cesare Stea. "Textile Industry." Terra cotta.

Cesare Stea. "Education." Plaster.

Relief

UP TO NOW MOST OF THE SCULPTURE METHODS DESCRIBED HAVE CONCERNED working in the full round. The knowledge and experience you have acquired will be helpful when creating a relief. There is seldom an armature problem, for unless the relief is very large, there will be no need for one. But whatever you have learned about the working properties and methods of clay, plaster, cement, wood, stone, and metal will apply when making a relief.

According to the dictionary, the term "relief" means a sculptured figure or design raised from a flat surface. There are some reliefs that are incised and so beneath the background surface. This is known as "intaglio." Then there are low reliefs commonly known as "bas-relief." The relief can be any depth, from very flat to medium to high (which can be almost full round, except that it is still set against a background).

A relief, which is a step between painting and sculpture in the round, can be far more pictorial than a sculptured block. It is a dimensional picture which creates the illusion of depth greater than it is. It can be decorative and flat with just a minimum of modeling, or a skillfully modeled or carved sculptured design either low, medium, or high in depth.

MODELING OR CARVING A RELIEF   Any sculpture medium can make a relief. It can be made of moist clay to be fired, or cast, or plasteline for casting. It can be carved in plaster, wood, or stone; or hammered in metal; or created with bricks, plastic metal, papier-mâché, or any other sculpture material.

Let us suppose you have a wall area that needs some decorative treatment. Perhaps a relief panel will be just the solution. You have a number of choices. One, you must decide on the subject or design; two, you determine whether the relief should be a modeled one, or carved; three, you select the material most suitable to both the subject and the setting. The source of light is important, for a relief will be most effective when viewed in the light for which it is intended. The wrong lighting can completely change the effect.

First, as always, plan your composition carefully. It can be drawn on paper, and enlarged the exact size of the relief. This can be traced or redrawn on the board or clay. Or better still, a small clay sketch can be made in proportion to the proposed relief. This can be very helpful when determining the depths of the various parts.

Clay is worked on a frame. This can be plywood or masonite, and should be painted with two or three coats of thin shellac. Some small nails put into the frame with the heads exposed will help hold the clay. The shellac will keep the board from warping or peeling when using moist clay, and prevent the board from absorbing the oil from the plasteline.

You may use several methods to make a relief, or you may prefer a combination of them. Either draw the design on the board, and then using the board as the background, build the forms within the designated area. Or build up a solid clay mass the desired thickness, flatten the surface, and with a modeling tool or nail draw the design on the clay. Then scoop away the background. The forms can be developed in the raised areas.

CASTING A RELIEF   A one-piece mold is usually enough for casting a clay relief. The mold process is very simple.

Lay the relief flat on its back and build a fence all around it. This can be a cardboard box, wood strips, or a wall of plasteline. The plaster is then mixed and poured directly over the clay forms to a thickness of about an inch. This can be reinforced with wire imbedded in the plaster, or burlap strips dipped in plaster.

The mold is treated with soap and oil as described on page 38.

Plaster can be poured into the mold, or cast-stone mixture can be pressed in.

You will probably want to hang the relief, so set a preformed wire hanger into the plaster or cement before it sets.

For a terra-cotta casting (which will have to be kiln fired), leave the plaster mold untreated, and pour clay slip or press clay into the mold.

Plaster will absorb the moisture from the wet clay and thus create a hard clay wall. Clay shrinks away from the plaster mold as it dries, so it practically separates itself.

If there are no undercuts in the plaster, the mold need not be chipped away. It can be lifted off, and several copies can be made if you wish. This is especially nice when you want to experiment with several patinas. If the plaster mold does not separate easily from the cast, tap it gently with a mallet.

A rubber mold can be used for casting; it is used to advantage only for quantity reproduction where undercuts are involved. The rubber mold must still have a plaster casing, to keep the forms from distorting, so a plaster mold in the first place seems more practical.

TO CARVE A RELIEF

In Plaster   Pour liquid plaster into a form. If the relief is small, a cardboard box cover can make a form. If larger, make a frame with wood strips and reinforce the back with wire and burlap. You will have to judge the requirements according to the size and weight of your relief.

When the plaster is well set, draw the design on it. The forms can be outlined with a small deep gouge, and the background is cut away. The forms can then be developed with plaster tools. When the finished relief is thoroughly dry, coat it with several coats of thin shellac and apply a patina.

In Wood Acquiring wood for a carved relief is often easier than getting logs or blocks for a full-round carving, for most lumber yards have carvable woods in plank size about an inch thick. The grain and color of wood make very handsome reliefs that fit into the *décor* of most contemporary living quarters, or enhance the walls of commercial establishments.

Draw the design of the relief on the wood. Scoop away the background with a gouge. Then develop the forms with your various wood-carving tools. Remember to keep your tools sharp, and always to cut with or across the grain. Never cut into the grain. An interesting contrast in texture can be achieved by leaving the background textured just as the tools leave it, and developing the forms of the relief to a fine polished finish.

In Stone Get your stone (marble or limestone) precut in clean slabs of the right dimensions. You can probably buy it or have it cut from a local tombstone maker, or from a mosaic-tile dealer where marble is sometimes sold for table tops. The background can be cut away with tooth chisels. Rasp and polish to reveal the delicacy of the forms.

When composing the relief, keep the figures in profile. Avoid a three-quarter view which presents problems in foreshortening.

Reliefs have a very important sculptural function. A sculptural panel can add an important decoration to a home. Indeed, it can be the center of interest. Architects incorporate sculptured panels into the designs of many contemporary buildings. Portraits are often done in relief, and medals and coins are executed by sculptors. So make experimenting with reliefs part of your sculptural experience.

TAKE INVENTORY

1. You have a place that needs a decorative point of interest.
2. The solution is a relief panel that not only will give you a chance to use your acquired sculptural skill, but can solve your decorative problem in a very personal way.
3. You have an idea and a design suitable for the area.
4. You must decide whether to model or carve the relief, and which material would be suitable for both the design and the setting.
5. The decision is made, so you get the necessary materials and tools.
6. You anticipate your pride in the finished product and the modest manner in which you will accept all praise.

IF YOU LIVE IN A METROPOLITAN AREA AND HAVE ACCESS TO THE VARIOUS museums and galleries, you will find that metal sculpture is appearing constantly and is now an accepted part of the sculpture scene.

Some of the metal sculpture is truly creative and ingenious. An artist who understands the scope of metal as a sculpture material and works within the limits of the material can produce some very exciting shapes and forms. Although metal does not have the warmth of wood or the elegance of stone, it has many working advantages. There is practically no limit to size. Metal can be made to look far more fragile than other materials, while actually it has great strength. Metal can be balanced more delicately. Some metals are made into sculpture by the combined processes of modeling and carving.

At the same time, under the guise of metal sculpture, there appear some tortuous, agonized bits of twisted metal, signed and titled, and because metal sculpture is a relatively new sculpture form, the viewing public is often afraid to admit that it might be poor sculpture. It does not matter how representative or how abstract a piece of sculpture is, nor does it matter what emotion or what message the sculpture tries to express. The important thing is, does it do it well, presenting the material and the forms in an expressive rhythmic manner? Do you react to the sculpture? Does it please you? Does it make you feel happy, amused, sad? If the sculpture gets the response from you that was intended, you can be reasonably sure it has merit.

As a viewer, approach all sculpture with an open mind. Let your honest reaction and good judgment determine the value of the sculpture to you.

Metal sculpture can be a very involved field. Its scope is enormous. The working equipment and materials can be frightening to a beginner. So going back to our original concept of this book, that sculpture is fun, and can be done by anyone who really wants to, I will present only a few of the simpler methods. Then if you find that metal sculpture seems to be your medium, you can get more information and more equipment.

Let us consider the working possibilities of metal.

Clay sculpture can be cast in various metals. This is a casting problem generally handed over to a commercial caster, so we will be concerned here only with metals for making sculpture directly.

Carl Milles. "Head of Orpheus." Iron. (*Courtesy of The Metropolitan Museum of Art. Purchase, Rogers Fund, 1940*)

Jose de Creeft. "Himalaya." Beaten lead. (*Collection of Whitney Museum of American Art, New York*)

HAMMERED METAL   Sculpture can be hammered out of sheets of metal. For this, lead which is soft and very malleable is best. Copper can also be hammered. The equipment is simple. All you need is a ball-peened hammer, a wooden mallet, and work gloves. Obtain sheets of lead or copper, as pure as possible, at a sheet-metal factory or art-supply dealer. Copper should be $\frac{1}{16}$-inch thick, while lead can be $\frac{1}{16}$- to $\frac{3}{8}$-inch thick. Copper has sharp edges, so tape the edges before starting, to prevent cutting yourself while handling. Gloves are always used when handling lead to prevent any possibility of lead poisoning. Large sheets of metal have to be suspended by clamps from the ceiling or by a pulley arrangement. However, I suggest your first ventures be small. Work against a sandbag on a bench or barrel.

A small clay sketch will help to place the design and judge the depth of forms. Draw the composition on the metal with chalk. You will have to redraw it many times while working, for the stretching metal will distort the drawing. Then, working from both the front and the back, and using the sandbags to hit against, with both the wood mallet and the hammer shape the forms freely. A small hammer, or any improvised tool, can shape the finer forms. Be careful not to thin the material too much, as in the case of a nose. Copper becomes hard and brittle after it has been hammered a while. It then has to be annealed, after which it becomes soft and malleable again. This is done by heating it with a blowtorch until it is dull red. Let it cool in the air. Clean the copper with a solution of vinegar and table salt before proceeding with the hammering. Lead needs no annealing.

The sculpture can be low relief, or almost full round. Lead is better for the full forms, while copper makes a fine sculpture of lower relief. Keep the design massive and simple. Don't try to get fine details.

When the piece is finished to your satisfaction, back it with a layer of cement. This will keep the forms from caving in, if hit accidentally. If there are no undercuts to hold the cement, create some with solder. Solder can also be used to back the more delicate thinned-out forms. Paint or spray lacquer on the back of the metal before putting on the cement. This will avoid any corrosive or chemical reaction.

The finished sculpture can be polished to a beautiful patina by rubbing it with steel wool and soap.

PLASTIC METAL   Several companies are now producing a metal that comes in a plastic putty form. The metal has its own solvent, so it can be diluted

to a soupy consistency. Thus the metal can be applied as clay, or brushed on over an armature or any previously prepared forms.

The material most available is aluminum. However, work is now in process to produce similar material in other metals, such as brass, copper, etc. In the meantime, the color of the aluminum can be varied by adding some bronzing powder to the final application. This plastic metal comes in cans. It is not inexpensive, but a little goes a long way. Also, because it produces a finished sculpture, the cost is reasonable. There are no casting or firing charges, and very few tools are necessary.

Plastic metal adheres to most any surface. So there are many ways to create with it. A simple wire armature as described earlier in the book (see pp. 22 ff.) can be made with any wire, as long as it will hold itself. The metal is put on in layers, and each layer must dry or set before the next layer is applied. Thus the armature acquires more strength and rigidity as it grows. This method is advisable only for a small piece, or if large, a thin, wiry concept. A sculpture with full forms built of solid masses of metal putty would be impractical. It would be too heavy and too expensive. When the forms are shaped over the armature and allowed to dry, the metal can then be filed, carved, sanded, and polished, if needed.

The unpolished metal is a dull silvery gray. This may be suitable for your sculpture just the way it is. But there is plenty of scope for improving the forms with files and tools, and the finished piece can be burnished to a beautiful luster by rubbing it with another metal such as with the back of a spoon.

For fuller forms, it is wise to create a hollow armature approximating the forms. The plastic metal is used to solidify the armature and to develop the forms. A hollow armature can be made with wire screening or hardware cloth. The shapes can be bound together with fine wire or solder. The metal is then coated over the wire armature, usually with a thinned solution of the material. When this is dry, the modeling can be completed and the work finished as described.

Because the metal adheres so well to many substances, you may enjoy the experience of combining metal with other materials to create an interesting, unusual sculpture. The metal can be combined with bits of stained glass effectively. Also think of the possibilities of combining with wood, semiprecious stones, shells, etc. This can be an excellent creative experience for a group of talented high-school students. And because the method is so simple and the space and equipment not demanding, it is a very good home project.

The metal can be applied with your fingers, a painting knife, a brush, etc., all of which can be washed in the solvent and not harmed.

Plastic metal can be bought from most sculpture-supply dealers.

FUSED METALS   The studios that are devoted to sculptors working with metals are beehives of activity. Sheets, rods, and bars of various metals are stacked about. Acetylene torches are blazing. Metal is welded to metal. Artists with protective garments, gloves, and face shields are busy creating new forms. This is what devotion to metal sculpture can lead to; but before embarking on anything so ambitious, there is much to be learned about the properties of metal.

Some of this experience can be gained by experimental sculpture with lead foil and a soldering iron.

The third method of metal sculpture that I will describe concerns working with melted metals. In essence, this is a matter of fusing metals together to create the shapes for sculpture.

You will need an armature, either wire or hollow. The only other equipment you will need will be:

1. A solder iron, purchased from an art store or hardware store.

2. Sheets of lead foil. (Sold by weight at a sculpture-supply dealer.)

3. Flux or soldering paste, which is used as a cleaning agent, and to help the fusing process of the metals. The metals must be clean to fuse.

With this minimum material and some imagination, many delightful small sculptures can be made.

The sheets of lead foil are crunched up and placed around the armature. With a hot solder iron, the outer surface of the lead foil is fused, thus leaving the sculpture light and airy. This is a continuous process.

Mobiles and Structures

MOBILES AND STRUCTURES ARE CONCERNED MORE WITH SPACE AND DESIGN THAN with form, but they are classified generally as sculpture. They are three-dimensional space designs which must be interesting and balanced from every possible view.

Making a mobile or a structure is a delightful experience. For young children, it is like playing with toys. Their uninhibited imagination will allow them to build with any available material, and to construct with an enviable intuitive sense of balance. Older children can plan a design with a theme, or just assemble abstract shapes in an interesting arrangement. They become conscious of the problems of balance, and can learn a very practical and valuable lesson. Adults can create serious and beautiful art objects. All the experience that has been acquired working with other sculpture forms (and drawing or painting)—a sense of rhythm, balance, texture, possibilities and limitations of materials—is employed to create a space design. The scope is unlimited. A complete list of tools and materials would be impossible.

Assemble the most obvious working equipment, such as a hammer, saw, pliers, tin snips, nails, glue, etc.

Some materials that can be used are cardboard, sheet metal, wire, glass, string, paper, wood, pipe cleaners, glass foam, plastic foam, hardware cloth, screening, feathers, cellophane, wooden dowels, toothpicks, cork, Christmas ornaments, etc., etc.

When you are ready to try a structure (with or without movement), assemble the materials most suitable to your idea and start working. Be experimental and imaginative.

A mobile is a structure that is suspended, and is made up of moving parts. It must be delicately balanced, so that any movement of air nearby will keep the mobile in motion. The shapes must be interesting from every view.

Since balance becomes one of the most important considerations, it is best to work with materials that are light in weight and that shape easily.

It is difficult to plan a mobile on paper, for the balance depends on both the weight of the objects that are hung and on their visual shapes. It is better, then, to start by suspending an arm from something high, such as a light fixture, a beam, or a rope stretched across the room. The arm can be wire, gracefully curved, or thin wooden dowels. Nylon fishing line is very

Alexander Calder. "Lobster Trap and Fish Tail. Mobile." Steel wire and sheet aluminum. (*Collection, The Museum of Modern Art, New York. Gift of the Advisory Committee*)

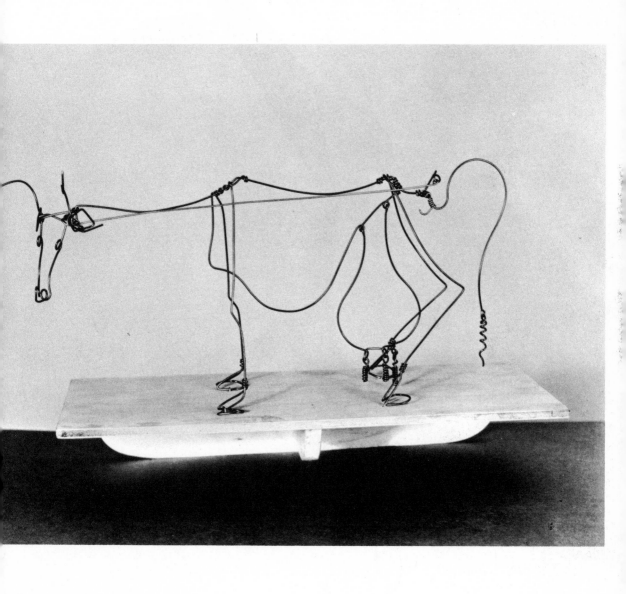

Alexander Calder. "Cow." Wire construction. (*Collection, The Museum of Modern Art, New York. Gift of Edward M. M. Warburg*)

Alexander Calder. "Whale. Stabile." (*Collection, The Museum of Modern Art, New York. Gift of the artist*)

Sue Fuller. "String Construction, Number 51." Plastic thread, aluminum. (*Collection of Whitney Museum of American Art, New York*)

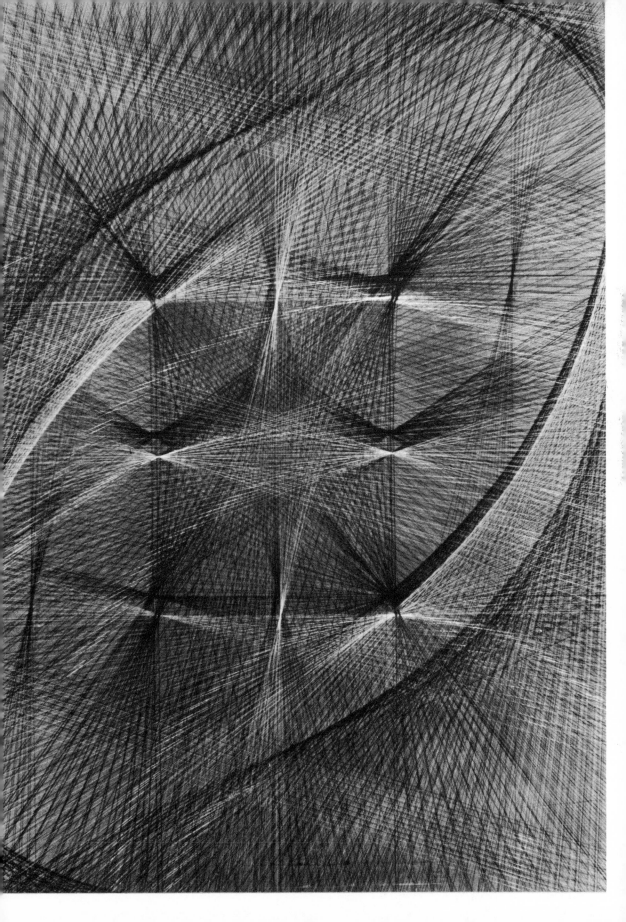

good for suspending the various arms and objects. It is strong and light, and gives free movement to the pieces. Several smaller arms can be suspended from the main arm and others from these, as long as they are balanced by an object or shape or possibly other suspended arms. Interesting shapes are suspended in such a way that they move freely as the air stirs.

Space may be a problem when making mobiles as a classroom project, because the mobiles must be suspended during the construction. A mobile has no meaning unless it is in space.

If there is not room to suspend the creative efforts of a group, make structures. The aim is the same and the problems similar. A structure is also a three-dimensional design in space, an imaginative construction of various materials arranged and balanced to be interesting from all views. Although sometimes movement is incorporated in it, the structure is a self-standing unit.

Since the structure must stand alone, start with a base. This base can be made of many things. Clay makes a good base for children, for they can insert objects freely, and the weight of the clay holds them down. Or the base can be wood. A rod or a dowel can be inserted into a hole drilled into the wood, so that it becomes the vertical support for the structure. You will have to invent your own method in most cases, for so many kinds of material can be used, and so many possible rhythms and designs, that the base and support will have to suit each individual project.

Structures and mobiles are particularly suitable projects for decorations related to many situations. They make charming Christmas decorations for the home, school, store-window displays, etc. Because they move, and because they can be suspended overhead, mobiles make good decorations for dances, fairs, parties, etc. An interesting structure can be very decorative in a home. If it is made weatherproof, it can add an important point of interest to a garden.

So try your hand at this contemporary art form. Do it for fun, for decoration, or for a serious art project. But try it—and prove that sculpture is fun!

Reference Books

GENERAL SCULPTURE INFORMATION

Zorach Explains Sculpture, by William Zorach. New York: Tudor Publishing Co., 1947.

The Materials and Methods of Sculpture, by Jack C. Rich. New York: Oxford University Press, Inc., 1947.

The Sculptor's Way, by Brenda Putnam. New York: Watson-Guptill Publications, Inc.

Creative Teaching in Art, by Victor D'Amico. Arts and Industries Series. Scranton, Pa.: International Textbook Co., 1953.

WOOD CARVING

Sculpture in Wood, by John Rood. Minneapolis: University of Minnesota Press, 1950.

Sculpture in Wood, by P. Edward Norman. New York: Studio Publications, Inc., 1954.

Wood Carving, by Alan Durst. New York: Studio Publications, Inc.

MOBILES AND STRUCTURES

How to Make Mobiles, by John Lynch. New York: The Viking Press, Inc., 1953.

Art for the Family, by Museum of Modern Art. New York: Doubleday & Company, Inc.

ANATOMY

Anatomical Diagrams for the Use of Art Students, by James M. Dunlop. New York: The Macmillan Co.

Constructive Anatomy, by George B. Bridgman. New York: Capitol Publishing Co., Inc.

Several of these books are out of print, but are available through your Public Library.

Where to Get Tools and Materials

SCULPTURE ASSOCIATES, 101 St. Marks Place, New York 9, New York
  All sculpture tools and materials, wood and stone.

STEWART CLAY CO., INC., 133 Mulberry Street, New York 13, New York
  Clay, plasteline, tools etc.

CRAFTOOLS, INC., 396 Broadway, New York 13, New York
  Clay and carving tools.

SCULPTURE HOUSE, 38 East 30th Street, New York 16, New York
  Tools and materials.

AMERICAN ART CLAY COMPANY, 4717 West 16th Street, Indianapolis, Indiana
  All kinds of clay and tools.

SCULP-METAL CO., 701-D Investment Building, Pittsburgh 22, Pennsylvania
  Metal in putty form.

J. H. MONTEATH LUMBER CO., 2500 Park Avenue, New York 51, New York
  Importers of hard woods.

WESTERN CERAMICS SUPPLY CO., 1601 Howard Street, San Francisco, California
  Clay and clay tools.

ADHESIVE PRODUCTS CORPORATION, 1660 Boone Avenue, New York 60, New York
  Rubber mold material.

POLYMER CHEMICAL COMPANY, 5920 Carthage Avenue, Cincinnati 12, Ohio
  Rubber mold material.